ANIMALS OF MASS DESTRUCTION

TENT CATERPILLARS

Gareth Stevens
PUBLISHING

By Barbara Linde

Please visit our website, www.garethstevens.com. For a free color catalog of all our high-quality books, call toll free 1-800-542-2595 or fax 1-877-542-2596.

Library of Congress Cataloging-in-Publication Data

Linde, Barbara M.
Tent caterpillars / by Barbara M. Linde.
p. cm. — (Animals of mass destruction)
Includes index.
ISBN 978-1-4824-1057-0 (pbk.)
ISBN 978-1-4824-1058-7 (6-pack)
ISBN 978-1-4824-1056-3 (library binding)
1. Tent caterpillars. 2. Caterpillars — Juvenile literature. I. Linde, Barbara M. II. Title.
QL544.2 L56 2015
 595.78—d23

First Edition

Published in 2015 by
Gareth Stevens Publishing
111 East 14th Street, Suite 349
New York, NY 10003

Copyright © 2015 Gareth Stevens Publishing

Designer: Andrea Davison-Bartolotta
Editor: Therese Shea

Photo credits: Cover, p. 1 (main) Photos Lamontagne/Photolibrary/Getty Images; cover, p. 1 (inset) Feng Yu/Shutterstock.com; series art (all textured backgrounds, yellow striped line) Elisanth/Shutterstock.com; series art (caption boxes) Fatseyeva/Shutterstock.com; series art (teal boxes) Tracie Andrews/Shutterstock.com; pp. 4-5, 16, 16-17 AdStock RF/Shutterstock.com; p. 5 (inset) Brandon Alms/Shutterstock.com; pp. 6-7 (main) Sari ONeal/Shutterstock.com; p. 7 (right inset) Tim Zurowski/All Canada Photos/Getty Images; p. 7 (left inset) Jessica Kuras/Shutterstock.com; p. 8 Robert L. Anderson/USDA Forest Service/Bugwood.org; pp. 8-9 Jerald E. Dewey/USDA Forest Service/Bugwood.org; pp. 10, 19 (inset) Whitney Cranshaw/Colorado State University/Bugwood.org; pp. 10-11 laura h/Shutterstock.com; p. 12 Dafinka/Shutterstock.com; pp. 12-13, 18 (tent caterpillar) Melinda Fawver/Shutterstock.com; p. 14 (apple tree) Potapov Alexander/Shutterstock.com; p. 14 (aspen) Maksym Bondarchuk/Shutterstock.com; pp. 14-15, 28-29 Johann Schumacher/Photolibrary/Getty Images; p. 18 (cycle) Olha Insight/Shutterstock.com; pp. 18-19 Nature's Images/Photo Researchers/Getty Images; p. 20 Marianne Fitzgerald/iStock/Thinkstock; pp. 20-21 Visuals Unlimited, Inc./Jeffrey Wickett/Getty Images; p. 22 Mike Watson Images/moodboard/Getty Images; pp. 22-23 Johann Schumacher/Oxford Scientific/Getty Images; p. 24 Tamara Kulikova/iStock/Thinkstock; pp. 24-25 Jan Samanek/State Phytosanitary Administration/Bugwood.org; pp. 26-27 Kallista Images/Getty Images.

Printed in the United States of America

CPSIA compliance information: Batch #CS15GS: For further information contact Gareth Stevens, New York, New York at 1-800-542-2595.

CONTENTS

Meet the Tent Caterpillars! 4

Where They Live. 6

Eggs. 8

Larvae 10

Pitching the Tent. 12

Out to Eat. 14

Messy Home 16

Pupae and Adults 18

Damaging Eating Habits 20

Attack of the Munchies. 22

Pesky Problems 24

Fighting Back 26

The Good Side. 28

Glossary. 30

For More Information. 31

Index 32

Words in the glossary appear in **bold** type the first time they are used in the text.

MEET THE TENT CATERPILLARS!

Have you ever seen a large, thick, white web in a tree? If so, you may have seen the tent of some tent caterpillars. In fact, you may have seen whole groups of trees covered with these silky webs. You can see them in a forest, a backyard, or even along city streets.

The white, silky webs might seem perfect for Halloween decorations, but don't be fooled! Tent caterpillars aren't helpful to people. In fact, their hunger for leaves can do great harm to trees.

Chew On This!

Early American colonists had problems with tent caterpillars. Massachusetts settlers called 1646 to 1649 the "caterpillar years."

tent caterpillar

Caterpillar tents can be different in size, but they always look white and silky like this.

WHERE THEY LIVE

There are 26 known kinds, or species, of tent caterpillars, including Sonoran tent caterpillars, forest tent caterpillars, and Pacific tent caterpillars.

Two of the worst pests, however, are eastern tent caterpillars and western tent caterpillars. They have a wide range, eat the leaves of many kinds of trees, and create the largest webbed tents. Eastern tent caterpillars live from southern Canada to the southeastern United States and from the East Coast to the Rocky Mountains. Western tent caterpillars are found mostly in the western United States, southern Canada, and northern Mexico.

Chew On This!

Forest tent caterpillars don't make tents! They eat a lot of leaves, though.

A caterpillar's markings help us tell species apart. The eastern tent caterpillar has a white stripe running down its back. The western tent caterpillar and forest tent caterpillar have dashes of white.

forest tent caterpillar

eastern tent caterpillar

western tent caterpillar

EGGS

The tent caterpillar begins its life cycle as an egg. The female tent caterpillar moth lays eggs in the summer. She lays a group of eggs, called an egg mass, about 1 inch (2.5 cm) long. That's about the size of your fingertip. However, it contains 150 to 350 eggs!

The moth wraps the egg mass around a tree branch that's about as thick as a pencil. The shiny, dark egg mass is covered with hard, glue-like matter to protect it.

eastern tent caterpillar egg mass

Chew On This!

Tent caterpillars lay eggs just once a year. That's a good thing. More eggs means more hungry caterpillars!

The matter the tent caterpillar moth covers the eggs with is called spumaline.

LARVAE

The egg mass stays on the branch for the rest of the summer, the fall, and the winter. The eggs hatch in the early spring, just as tree leaves are beginning to grow. Young caterpillars, called **larvae**, come out. They're hungry and **destructive**!

First, the larvae chew their way out of the eggs. Then, they eat the hard coating of the egg mass. Next, they start eating young tree leaves. Since they live in trees, tent caterpillars have plenty of food close by.

After hatching, caterpillars from one egg mass may join another group.

PITCHING THE TENT

After tent caterpillars hatch, they head to where the tree branch meets the trunk of the tree. Together, they begin to construct their "tent" from silk they make in their body. As the caterpillars grow, they make their tent larger. If you see a lot of tent caterpillars crawling on the outside of the tent, they're weaving another layer.

The tent is quite strong. It protects the tent caterpillars from heat, cold, wind, and rain. It keeps them safe from some predators, too.

Chew On This!

There are anywhere from 50 to 200 caterpillars in an eastern tent caterpillar colony. That's a lot of hungry caterpillars!

The eastern tent caterpillar builds one of the largest tents of any tent caterpillar.

13

OUT TO EAT

Caterpillars stay in or on the tent except when they're feeding—which is several times a day! This is the life stage when tent caterpillars do the most **damage** to trees by eating their leaves.

Scientists have discovered that a tent caterpillar leaves a scent, or smell, on its path so other members of the colony can find food. Some even think the caterpillar tells others just how good the leaves taste with this scent!

Chew On This!

Eastern tent caterpillars like apple, wild cherry, and crab apple trees. The aspen is a favorite tree for western tent caterpillars. Sonoran and Pacific tent caterpillars like oak trees.

apple tree

aspen

Younger, smaller caterpillars eat during the daytime. They stay in the tent at night. The older, larger caterpillars do the opposite.

MESSY HOME

As they eat leaves and grow larger, the caterpillars **shed** their outer skin inside the tent. They do this four or five times in the larva stage. They also leave waste matter, or frass, in the tent. The tent starts looking old and dirty.

After about 6 weeks, the caterpillars are fully grown. They leave the tent. An ugly web is left on the tree. While it doesn't harm the trees, it isn't pretty to look at.

You can see the frass in this caterpillar tent.

Chew On This!

Caterpillars may move from place to place in the tent to warm up or cool down.

17

PUPAE AND ADULTS

After leaving the nest for the last time, a tent caterpillar attaches itself to a tree, building, rock, or even a fence. It spins a silk cocoon around its body. This form of the insect is called the **pupa**. The pupa grows and changes inside the cocoon.

An adult moth comes out of the cocoon 2 to 4 weeks later. It only lives for about 5 days! During that time, the male and female moths **mate**. Then, the female lays the egg mass. The cycle starts again.

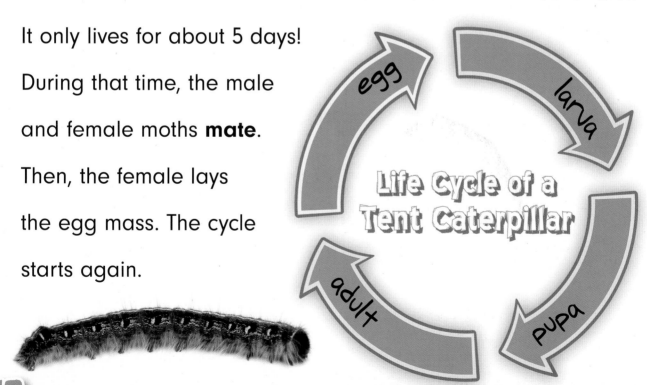

Life Cycle of a Tent Caterpillar

egg

larva

pupa

adult

The yellowish-white tent caterpillar cocoon is about 1 inch (2.5 cm) long.

DAMAGING EATING HABITS

A tree's leaves collect energy from the sun and make **nutrients** that a tree needs to live. Large, healthy trees can usually survive a tent caterpillar colony, though the loss of leaves can slow growth. It might even be able to grow more leaves that year. However, a smaller or unhealthy tree may die with just one colony eating its leaves.

If caterpillars eat too many of the leaves of fruit trees, the trees may not be able to produce the tasty fruits people and animals like to eat.

These trees in Huron-Manistee National Forest in Michigan were **infested** with tent caterpillars. Can you tell by the lack of leaves?

ATTACK OF THE MUNCHIES

Most of the time, a group of caterpillars stays on its home tree. One tree usually provides enough food for the colony. But when the colony is large, or there aren't enough leaves, the group infests other nearby trees. These pests can affect whole forests or neighborhoods.

Sometimes caterpillars feast on the same trees year after year. When this happens, healthy trees weaken and die.

Chew On This!

Predators play an important role in keeping tent caterpillar numbers in check. Without birds, bats, and other animals that eat caterpillars, more trees would die.

Tent caterpillars can make beautiful trees look ugly.

PESKY PROBLEMS

Because of their ugly nests and harmful leaf munching, people think of tent caterpillars as destructive pests. Sometimes, too, caterpillars make tents on picnic tables, fences, and outdoor furniture. The insects may drop from trees and land on people, buildings, plants, and cars. They can cover sidewalks and streets. Yuck!

Once the tent caterpillar moths hatch, they can crowd around porch lights. It's not as pleasant spending time outside when you're surrounded by caterpillars and moths!

24

Hundreds of tent caterpillars dropping in for a visit in your tent can spoil a campout!

FIGHTING BACK

So, how do people get rid of tent caterpillars? Some **prune** branches that have egg masses on them. Others use a knife to scrape the eggs off. If the caterpillars have already made a tent, you can blast the tent with water or knock it down with a stick.

Some people use **insecticides** to kill tent caterpillars. However, insecticides can damage leaves, so they should be used carefully.

Other people spray vegetable oil or soapy water on nests. These can coat the caterpillars' skin so they can't breathe.

Chew On This!

Some people pick caterpillars out of trees. However, their tiny hairs may bother a person's skin. It's a good idea to wear gloves when doing this.

Some wasps lay their eggs on tent caterpillars. When the eggs hatch, the young wasps eat the caterpillars.

THE GOOD SIDE

Many people just leave tent caterpillars alone. In some ways, they're an important part of their **ecosystem**. Birds use their sharp beaks to rip open tents and eat caterpillars. Some birds and bats also eat cocoons and moths.

Frass and dead caterpillars **fertilize** soil, helping it to become healthy for new plants. Tent caterpillars are pests, but they aren't all bad!

Tent Caterpillars: Ecosystem Pests or Partners?

pests	partners
eat tree leaves	fertilize the soil
weave ugly tents	provide light for plants under trees
build nests on people's property	food for birds, bats, and others
prevent fruit from growing	wasp larvae hatch on and eat caterpillars

This cuckoo is chowing down on tent caterpillars.

Chew On This!

When caterpillars eat leaves, plants below the trees get more sunlight and are able to grow better.

29

GLOSSARY

damage: harm. Also, to cause harm.

destructive: very harmful

ecosystem: all the living things in an area

fertilize: to make soil better for growing crops and other plants

infest: to overrun a place in large numbers and become harmful or unpleasant

insecticide: a substance used to kill insects

larva: a bug in an early life stage that has a wormlike form. The plural form is "larvae."

mate: to come together to make babies

nutrient: something a living thing needs to grow and stay alive

prune: to cut branches off a plant to help it grow better or to give it a better shape

pupa: a bug that is changing from a larva to an adult, usually inside a case or cocoon. The plural form is "pupae."

shed: to lose skin, hair, or fur

FOR MORE INFORMATION

Books

Bishop, Nic. *Forest Explorer: A Life-Size Field Guide*. New York, NY: Scholastic Press, 2004.

Jackson, Cari. *Bugs That Build*. New York, NY: Marshall Cavendish Benchmark, 2009.

Wagner, David L. *Caterpillars of Eastern North America: A Guide to Identification and Natural History*. Princeton, NJ: Princeton University Press, 2005.

Websites

Eastern Tent Caterpillar Moth
animaldiversity.ummz.umich.edu/site/accounts/information/Malacosoma_americanum.html
Read about the life cycle of the eastern tent caterpillar as well as its role in the ecosystem.

Tent Caterpillars
www2.ca.uky.edu/entomology/entfacts/ef424.asp
Read quick tips about how to get rid of these creatures and other tree dwellers.

Western Tent Caterpillars
www.fs.fed.us/r3/resources/health/field-guide/fid/tent-caterpillar.shtml
See photos of these pests in several stages of their life cycle.

INDEX

cocoon 18, 19, 28

colony 12, 14, 20, 22

eastern tent caterpillar 6, 7, 12, 13, 14

ecosystem 28

egg mass 8, 10, 11, 18, 26

eggs 8, 9, 10, 26, 27

fertilize 28

frass 16, 17, 28

insecticides 26

larvae 10, 16, 28

leaves 4, 6, 10, 14, 16, 20, 21, 22, 24, 26, 28, 29

predators 12, 22

prune trees 26

pupa 18

shed 16

silk 12, 18

soapy water 26

species 6, 7

tent caterpillar moth 8, 9, 18, 24, 28

tents 4, 5, 6, 12, 13, 14, 15, 16, 17, 24, 26, 28

trees 4, 6, 8, 10, 12, 14, 16, 18, 20, 21, 22, 23, 24, 26, 28, 29

vegetable oil 26

wasps 27, 28

webs 4, 6, 16

western tent caterpillar 6, 7, 14